CW00382803

BOOK CLUB

JOURNAL

All rights reserved.
This book or any portion thereof
may not be reproduced or used in any manner whatsoever
without the express written permission of the publisher
except for the use of brief quotations in a book review.
Copyright © 2021 by Select Publishing Ltd
www.notebookandjournal.com

Contents

Book Club Reads

TITLE   SCORE

1 _____   ◯

   by _____

2 _____   ◯

   by _____

3 _____   ◯

   by _____

4 _____   ◯

   by _____

5 _____   ◯

   by _____

6 _____   ◯

   by _____

Reasons to Love Book Club

Reading a new book a month and finishing it.

Reading books I wouldn't normally read.

Discovering books that might make me laugh or cry.

Having people to talk to when I finish a book, who have also read it.

Book Club Reads

TITLE	SCORE
7 _____	
by _____	
8 _____	
by _____	
9 _____	
by _____	
10 _____	
by _____	
11 _____	
by _____	
12 _____	
by _____	

Reasons to Love Book Club

Engaging in heated debates.

Having long and thoughtful discussions.

Agreeing about good or bad stories and wonderful or terrible

characters.

Meeting friends regularly, enjoying the company of

interesting people.

Book Club Reads

TITLE   SCORE

13 _____   ◯

by _____

14 _____   ◯

by _____

15 _____   ◯

by _____

16 _____   ◯

by _____

17 _____   ◯

by _____

18 _____   ◯

by _____

Reasons to Love Book Club

Coffee and cake.

Red wine....white wine.. all wine.

And finally catching up with friends to talk about

our lives,

local news, TV, films and more books.

Book Club Reads

TITLE   SCORE

19 _____   ◯

by _____

20 _____   ◯

by _____

21 _____   ◯

by _____

22 _____   ◯

by _____

23 _____   ◯

by _____

24 _____   ◯

by _____

BOOK 1

Title

_____

_____
(Year of publication & page count)

Author

_____

Meeting Month/Year

_____

Meeting Day/Date

_____

Book Chosen By

_____

Meeting Place/Time

_____

———◁◆▷———

Where is the book set? _____

And in what era? _____

What are the main themes/genre of the book?

_____

_____

_____

Notes: notable characters, your thoughts and ease of reading.

_____

_____

_____

_____

_____

Brief summary

_____

_____

_____

_____

_____

_____

How did it end ?

_____

_____

_____

_____

My Review - Score Out of 10

☆ ☆ ☆ ☆ ☆ ☆ ☆ ☆ ☆ ☆

1. How much did you enjoy the book?	/10
2. Would you read something else by this author?	/10
3. Would you recommend the book?	/10
4. Did it create an interesting discussion?	/10
My Total Score:	/40

Book club rated this book :

BOOK 2

Title

_____

_____
(Year of publication & page count)

Author

_____

Meeting Month/Year

_____

Meeting Day/Date

_____

Book Chosen By

_____

Meeting Place/Time

_____

Where is the book set? _____

And in what era? _____

What are the main themes/genre of the book?

_____

_____

_____

Notes: notable characters, your thoughts and ease of reading.

_____

_____

_____

_____

_____

Brief summary

_____

_____

_____

_____

_____

_____

How did it end ?

_____

_____

_____

_____

My Review - Score Out of 10
☆ ☆ ☆ ☆ ☆ ☆ ☆ ☆ ☆ ☆

1. How much did you enjoy the book?	/10
2. Would you read something else by this author?	/10
3. Would you recommend the book?	/10
4. Did it create an interesting discussion?	/10
My Total Score:	/40

Book club rated this book :

BOOK 3

Title

_____

_____
(Year of publication & page count)

Author

_____

Meeting Month/Year

_____

Meeting Day/Date

_____

Book Chosen By

_____

Meeting Place/Time

_____

Where is the book set? _____

And in what era? _____

What are the main themes/genre of the book?

_____

_____

_____

Notes: notable characters, your thoughts and ease of reading.

_____

_____

_____

_____

_____

Brief summary

_____
_____
_____
_____
_____
_____

How did it end ?

_____
_____
_____
_____

My Review - Score Out of 10
☆ ☆ ☆ ☆ ☆ ☆ ☆ ☆ ☆ ☆

1. How much did you enjoy the book?	/10
2. Would you read something else by this author?	/10
3. Would you recommend the book?	/10
4. Did it create an interesting discussion?	/10
My Total Score:	/40

Book club rated this book :

BOOK
4

Title

_____

_____
(Year of publication & page count)

Author

_____

Meeting Month/Year

_____

Meeting Day/Date

_____

Book Chosen By

_____

Meeting Place/Time

_____

Where is the book set? _____

And in what era? _____

What are the main themes/genre of the book?

_____

_____

_____

Notes: notable characters, your thoughts and ease of reading.

_____

_____

_____

_____

_____

Brief summary

_____

_____

_____

_____

_____

_____

How did it end ?

_____

_____

_____

_____

My Review - Score Out of 10
☆ ☆ ☆ ☆ ☆ ☆ ☆ ☆ ☆ ☆

1. How much did you enjoy the book?   /10

2. Would you read something else by this author?   /10

3. Would you recommend the book?   /10

4. Did it create an interesting discussion?   /10

My Total Score: /40

Book club rated this book :

BOOK 5

Title

_____

_____
(Year of publication & page count)

Author

_____

Meeting Month/Year

_____

Meeting Day/Date

_____

Book Chosen By

_____

Meeting Place/Time

_____

Where is the book set? _____

And in what era? _____

What are the main themes/genre of the book?

_____

_____

_____

Notes: notable characters, your thoughts and ease of reading.

_____

_____

_____

_____

_____

Brief summary

_____

_____

_____

_____

_____

_____

How did it end ?

_____

_____

_____

My Review - Score Out of 10
☆ ☆ ☆ ☆ ☆ ☆ ☆ ☆ ☆ ☆

1. How much did you enjoy the book?   / 10

2. Would you read something else by this author?   / 10

3. Would you recommend the book?   / 10

4. Did it create an interesting discussion?   / 10

My Total Score: / 40

Book club rated this book :

BOOK 6

Title

_____

_____
(Year of publication & page count)

Author

_____

Meeting Month/Year

_____

Meeting Day/Date

_____

Book Chosen By

_____

Meeting Place/Time

_____

⊲◆▷

Where is the book set? _____

And in what era? _____

What are the main themes/genre of the book?

_____

_____

_____

Notes: notable characters, your thoughts and ease of reading.

_____

_____

_____

_____

_____

Brief summary

_____

_____

_____

_____

_____

_____

How did it end ?

_____

_____

_____

_____

My Review - Score Out of 10
☆ ☆ ☆ ☆ ☆ ☆ ☆ ☆ ☆ ☆

1. How much did you enjoy the book?	/10
2. Would you read something else by this author?	/10
3. Would you recommend the book?	/10
4. Did it create an interesting discussion?	/10
My Total Score:	/40

Book club rated this book :

BOOK 7

Title

_____

_____
(Year of publication & page count)

Author

_____

Meeting Month/Year

_____

Meeting Day/Date

_____

Book Chosen By

_____

Meeting Place/Time

_____

————⊲◆⊳————

Where is the book set? _____

And in what era? _____

What are the main themes/genre of the book?

_____

_____

_____

Notes: notable characters, your thoughts and ease of reading.

_____

_____

_____

_____

_____

Brief summary

_____

_____

_____

_____

_____

_____

How did it end ?

_____

_____

_____

_____

My Review - Score Out of 10

☆ ☆ ☆ ☆ ☆ ☆ ☆ ☆ ☆ ☆

1. How much did you enjoy the book?	/10
2. Would you read something else by this author?	/10
3. Would you recommend the book?	/10
4. Did it create an interesting discussion?	/10
My Total Score:	/40

Book club rated this book :

BOOK 8

Title

_____

_____
(Year of publication & page count)

Author

_____

Meeting Month/Year

_____

Meeting Day/Date

_____

Book Chosen By

_____

Meeting Place/Time

_____

Where is the book set? _____

And in what era? _____

What are the main themes/genre of the book?

_____

_____

_____

Notes: notable characters, your thoughts and ease of reading.

_____

_____

_____

_____

_____

Brief summary

_____
_____
_____
_____
_____
_____

How did it end ?

_____
_____
_____
_____

My Review - Score Out of 10
☆ ☆ ☆ ☆ ☆ ☆ ☆ ☆ ☆ ☆

1. How much did you enjoy the book?   /10
2. Would you read something else by this author?   /10
3. Would you recommend the book?   /10
4. Did it create an interesting discussion?   /10

                              My Total Score: /40

Book club rated this book :

BOOK
9

Title

_____

_____
(Year of publication & page count)

Author

_____

Meeting Month/Year

_____

Meeting Day/Date

_____

Book Chosen By

_____

Meeting Place/Time

_____

Where is the book set? _____

And in what era? ___ _____

What are the main themes/genre of the book?

_____

_____

_____

Notes: notable characters, your thoughts and ease of reading.

_____

_____

_____

_____

_____

Brief summary

_____

_____

_____

_____

_____

_____

How did it end ?

_____

_____

_____

_____

My Review - Score Out of 10
☆ ☆ ☆ ☆ ☆ ☆ ☆ ☆ ☆ ☆

1. How much did you enjoy the book?   /10

2. Would you read something else by this author?   /10

3. Would you recommend the book?   /10

4. Did it create an interesting discussion?   /10

My Total Score: /40

Book club rated this book :

BOOK 10

Title

_____

_____
(Year of publication & page count)

Author

_____

Meeting Month/Year

_____

Meeting Day/Date

_____

Book Chosen By

_____

Meeting Place/Time

_____

—◁◆▷—

Where is the book set? _____

And in what era? _____

What are the main themes/genre of the book?

_____

_____

_____

Notes: notable characters, your thoughts and ease of reading.

_____

_____

_____

_____

_____

Brief summary

_____

_____

_____

_____

_____

_____

How did it end ?

_____

_____

_____

_____

My Review - Score Out of 10
☆ ☆ ☆ ☆ ☆ ☆ ☆ ☆ ☆ ☆

1. How much did you enjoy the book?   /10

2. Would you read something else by this author?   /10

3. Would you recommend the book?   /10

4. Did it create an interesting discussion?   /10

My Total Score: /40

Book club rated this book :

BOOK

11

Title

_____

_____
(Year of publication & page count)

Author

_____

Meeting Month/Year

_____

Meeting Day/Date

_____

Book Chosen By

_____

Meeting Place/Time

_____

Where is the book set? _____

And in what era? _____

What are the main themes/genre of the book?

_____

_____

_____

Notes: notable characters, your thoughts and ease of reading.

_____

_____

_____

_____

_____

Brief summary

_____

_____

_____

_____

_____

_____

How did it end ?

_____

_____

_____

_____

My Review - Score Out of 10
☆ ☆ ☆ ☆ ☆ ☆ ☆ ☆ ☆ ☆

1. How much did you enjoy the book?   /10

2. Would you read something else by this author?   /10

3. Would you recommend the book?   /10

4. Did it create an interesting discussion?   /10

My Total Score: /40

Book club rated this book :

BOOK

12

Title

_____

_____
(Year of publication & page count)

Author

_____

Meeting Month/Year

_____

Meeting Day/Date

_____

Book Chosen By

_____

Meeting Place/Time

_____

———◁◆▷———

Where is the book set? _____

And in what era? _____

What are the main themes/genre of the book?

_____

_____

_____

Notes: notable characters, your thoughts and ease of reading.

_____

_____

_____

_____

_____

Brief summary

_____

_____

_____

_____

_____

_____

How did it end ?

_____

_____

_____

_____

My Review - Score Out of 10
☆ ☆ ☆ ☆ ☆ ☆ ☆ ☆ ☆ ☆

1. How much did you enjoy the book?	/10
2. Would you read something else by this author?	/10
3. Would you recommend the book?	/10
4. Did it create an interesting discussion?	/10
My Total Score:	/40

Book club rated this book :

BOOK

13

Title

_____

_____
               (Year of publication & page count)

Author

_____

Meeting Month/Year

_____

Book Chosen By

_____

Meeting Day/Date

_____

Meeting Place/Time

_____

⊲◆⊳

Where is the book set? _____

And in what era? _____

What are the main themes/genre of the book?

_____

_____

_____

Notes: notable characters, your thoughts and ease of reading.

_____

_____

_____

_____

_____

Brief summary

_____

_____

_____

_____

_____

_____

How did it end ?

_____

_____

_____

_____

My Review - Score Out of 10
☆ ☆ ☆ ☆ ☆ ☆ ☆ ☆ ☆ ☆

1. How much did you enjoy the book?   /10
2. Would you read something else by this author?   /10
3. Would you recommend the book?   /10
4. Did it create an interesting discussion?   /10

              My Total Score: /40

Book club rated this book :

BOOK 14

Title

_____

_____
(Year of publication & page count)

Author

_____

Meeting Month/Year

_____

Meeting Day/Date

_____

Book Chosen By

_____

Meeting Place/Time

_____

———◁◆▷———

Where is the book set? _____

And in what era? _____

What are the main themes/genre of the book?

_____

_____

_____

Notes: notable characters, your thoughts and ease of reading.

_____

_____

_____

_____

_____

Brief summary

_____

_____

_____

_____

_____

_____

How did it end ?

_____

_____

_____

_____

My Review - Score Out of 10
☆ ☆ ☆ ☆ ☆ ☆ ☆ ☆ ☆ ☆

1. How much did you enjoy the book?   /10

2. Would you read something else by this author?   /10

3. Would you recommend the book?   /10

4. Did it create an interesting discussion?   /10

My Total Score: /40

Book club rated this book :

BOOK 15

Title

_____

_____
(Year of publication & page count)

Author

_____

Meeting Month/Year

_____

Meeting Day/Date

_____

Book Chosen By

_____

Meeting Place/Time

_____

Where is the book set? _____

And in what era? _____

What are the main themes/genre of the book?

_____

_____

_____

Notes: notable characters, your thoughts and ease of reading.

_____

_____

_____

_____

_____

Brief summary

_____

_____

_____

_____

_____

_____

How did it end ?

_____

_____

_____

_____

My Review - Score Out of 10
☆ ☆ ☆ ☆ ☆ ☆ ☆ ☆ ☆ ☆

1. How much did you enjoy the book?   /10
2. Would you read something else by this author?   /10
3. Would you recommend the book?   /10
4. Did it create an interesting discussion?   /10

My Total Score: /40

Book club rated this book :

BOOK 16

Title

_____

_____
(Year of publication & page count)

Author

_____

Meeting Month/Year

_____

Meeting Day/Date

_____

Book Chosen By

_____

Meeting Place/Time

_____

Where is the book set? _____

And in what era? _____

What are the main themes/genre of the book?

_____

_____

_____

Notes: notable characters, your thoughts and ease of reading.

_____

_____

_____

_____

_____

Brief summary

_____

_____

_____

_____

_____

_____

How did it end ?

_____

_____

_____

_____

My Review - Score Out of 10
☆ ☆ ☆ ☆ ☆ ☆ ☆ ☆ ☆ ☆

1. How much did you enjoy the book?   /10

2. Would you read something else by this author?   /10

3. Would you recommend the book?   /10

4. Did it create an interesting discussion?   /10

My Total Score: /40

Book club rated this book :

BOOK 17

Title

_____

_____
(Year of publication & page count)

Author

_____

Meeting Month/Year

_____

Meeting Day/Date

_____

Book Chosen By

_____

Meeting Place/Time

_____

———◁◆▷———

Where is the book set? _____

And in what era? _____

What are the main themes/genre of the book?

_____

_____

_____

Notes: notable characters, your thoughts and ease of reading.

_____

_____

_____

_____

_____

Brief summary

_____

_____

_____

_____

_____

_____

How did it end ?

_____

_____

_____

_____

My Review - Score Out of 10
☆ ☆ ☆ ☆ ☆ ☆ ☆ ☆ ☆ ☆

1. How much did you enjoy the book?   /10

2. Would you read something else by this author?   /10

3. Would you recommend the book?   /10

4. Did it create an interesting discussion?   /10

My Total Score: /40

Book club rated this book :

BOOK 18

Title

_____

_____
(Year of publication & page count)

Author

_____

Meeting Month/Year

_____

Meeting Day/Date

_____

Book Chosen By

_____

Meeting Place/Time

_____

Where is the book set? _____

And in what era? _____

What are the main themes/genre of the book?

_____

_____

_____

Notes: notable characters, your thoughts and ease of reading.

_____

_____

_____

_____

_____

Brief summary

_____

_____

_____

_____

_____

_____

How did it end ?

_____

_____

_____

_____

My Review - Score Out of 10

☆ ☆ ☆ ☆ ☆ ☆ ☆ ☆ ☆ ☆

1. How much did you enjoy the book?	/10
2. Would you read something else by this author?	/10
3. Would you recommend the book?	/10
4. Did it create an interesting discussion?	/10
My Total Score:	/40

Book club rated this book :

BOOK
19

Title

_____

_____
(Year of publication & page count)

Author

_____

Meeting Month/Year

_____

Meeting Day/Date

_____

Book Chosen By

_____

Meeting Place/Time

_____

⊲◆⊳

Where is the book set? _____

And in what era? _____

What are the main themes/genre of the book?

_____

_____

_____

Notes: notable characters, your thoughts and ease of reading.

_____

_____

_____

_____

_____

Brief summary

_____

_____

_____

_____

_____

_____

How did it end ?

_____

_____

_____

_____

My Review - Score Out of 10

☆ ☆ ☆ ☆ ☆ ☆ ☆ ☆ ☆ ☆

1. How much did you enjoy the book?	/10
2. Would you read something else by this author?	/10
3. Would you recommend the book?	/10
4. Did it create an interesting discussion?	/10
My Total Score:	/40

Book club rated this book :

BOOK 20

Title

_____

_____
(Year of publication & page count)

Author

_____

Meeting Month/Year

_____

Meeting Day/Date

_____

Book Chosen By

_____

Meeting Place/Time

_____

⟨◆⟩

Where is the book set? _____

And in what era? _____

What are the main themes/genre of the book?

_____

_____

_____

Notes: notable characters, your thoughts and ease of reading.

_____

_____

_____

_____

_____

Brief summary

_____

_____

_____

_____

_____

_____

How did it end ?

_____

_____

_____

_____

My Review - Score Out of 10

☆ ☆ ☆ ☆ ☆ ☆ ☆ ☆ ☆ ☆

1. How much did you enjoy the book?   /10
2. Would you read something else by this author?   /10
3. Would you recommend the book?   /10
4. Did it create an interesting discussion?   /10

My Total Score: /40

Book club rated this book :

BOOK 21

Title

_____

_____
(Year of publication & page count)

Author

_____

Meeting Month/Year

_____

Meeting Day/Date

_____

Book Chosen By

_____

Meeting Place/Time

_____

Where is the book set? _____

And in what era? _____

What are the main themes/genre of the book?

_____

_____

_____

Notes: notable characters, your thoughts and ease of reading.

_____

_____

_____

_____

_____

Brief summary

_____

_____

_____

_____

_____

_____

How did it end ?

_____

_____

_____

_____

My Review - Score Out of 10
☆ ☆ ☆ ☆ ☆ ☆ ☆ ☆ ☆ ☆

1. How much did you enjoy the book?   /10
2. Would you read something else by this author?   /10
3. Would you recommend the book?   /10
4. Did it create an interesting discussion?   /10

My Total Score: /40

Book club rated this book :

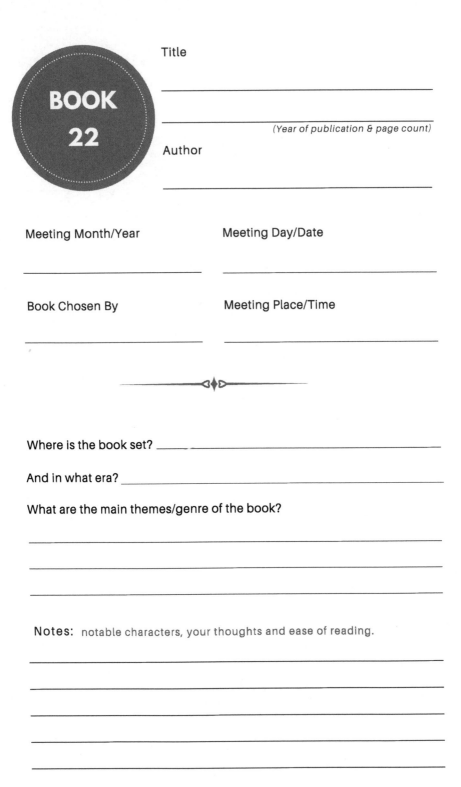

BOOK 22

Title

_____

_____
(Year of publication & page count)

Author

_____

Meeting Month/Year

_____

Meeting Day/Date

_____

Book Chosen By

_____

Meeting Place/Time

_____

Where is the book set? _____

And in what era? _____

What are the main themes/genre of the book?

_____

_____

_____

Notes: notable characters, your thoughts and ease of reading.

_____

_____

_____

_____

_____

Brief summary

_____

_____

_____

_____

_____

_____

How did it end ?

_____

_____

_____

_____

My Review - Score Out of 10

☆ ☆ ☆ ☆ ☆ ☆ ☆ ☆ ☆ ☆

1. How much did you enjoy the book?	/10
2. Would you read something else by this author?	/10
3. Would you recommend the book?	/10
4. Did it create an interesting discussion?	/10
My Total Score:	/40

Book club rated this book :

BOOK 23

Title

_____

_____
(Year of publication & page count)

Author

_____

Meeting Month/Year

_____

Meeting Day/Date

_____

Book Chosen By

_____

Meeting Place/Time

_____

Where is the book set? _____

And in what era? _____

What are the main themes/genre of the book?

_____

_____

_____

Notes: notable characters, your thoughts and ease of reading.

_____

_____

_____

_____

_____

Brief summary

_____

_____

_____

_____

_____

_____

How did it end ?

_____

_____

_____

_____

My Review - Score Out of 10

☆ ☆ ☆ ☆ ☆ ☆ ☆ ☆ ☆ ☆

1. How much did you enjoy the book?	/10
2. Would you read something else by this author?	/10
3. Would you recommend the book?	/10
4. Did it create an interesting discussion?	/10
My Total Score:	/40

Book club rated this book :

BOOK 24

Title

_____

_____
(Year of publication & page count)

Author

_____

Meeting Month/Year

_____

Meeting Day/Date

_____

Book Chosen By

_____

Meeting Place/Time

_____

Where is the book set? _____

And in what era? _____

What are the main themes/genre of the book?

_____

_____

_____

Notes: notable characters, your thoughts and ease of reading.

_____

_____

_____

_____

_____

Brief summary

_____

_____

_____

_____

_____

_____

How did it end ?

_____

_____

_____

_____

My Review - Score Out of 10

☆ ☆ ☆ ☆ ☆ ☆ ☆ ☆ ☆ ☆

1. How much did you enjoy the book?	/10
2. Would you read something else by this author?	/10
3. Would you recommend the book?	/10
4. Did it create an interesting discussion?	/10
My Total Score:	/40

Book club rated this book :

Notes

Notes

Notes

Notes

Notes

Notes

Notes

Notes

Notes

Notes

Notes

Notes

Notes

Notes

Notes

Notes

Notes

POPULAR
BOOK CLUB
BOOKS

Book Recommendations

The Help
by Kathryn Stockett

Gone Girl
by Gillian Flynn

Educated
by Tara Westover

The Book Thief
by Markus Zusak

A Man Called Ove
by Fredrik Backman

Little Fires Everywhere
by Celeste Ng

The Girl on the Train
by Paula Hawkins

Eleanor Oliphant Is Completely Fine
by Gail Honeyman

The Light Between Oceans
by M.L. Stedman

The Immortal Life of Henrietta Lacks
by Rebecca Skloot

The Nightingale
by Kristin Hannah

The Glass Castle
by Jeannette Walls

The Night Circus
by Erin Morgenstern

Where'd You Go, Bernadette
by Maria Semple

Me Before You
by Jojo Moyes

The Rosie Project
by Graeme Simsion

Water for Elephants
by Sara Gruen

The Handmaid's Tale
by Margaret Atwood

Room
by Emma Donoghue

Before We Were Yours
by Lisa Wingate

A Gentleman in Moscow
by Amor Towles

Wild
by Cheryl Strayed

The Husband's Secret
by Liane Moriarty

The Invention of Wings
by Sue Monk Kidd

Orphan Train
by Christina Baker Kline

Book Recommendations

Cutting for Stone
by Abraham Verghese

Big Little Lies
by Liane Moriarty

The Goldfinch
by Donna Tartt

The Language of Flowers
by Vanessa Diffenbaugh

Sarah's Key
by Tatiana de Rosnay

The Fault in Our Stars
by John Green

The Paris Wife
by Paula McLain

**Hotel on the Corner of Bitter
and Sweet**
by Jamie Ford

Station Eleven
by Emily St. John Mandel

The Art of Racing in the Rain
by Garth Stein

Still Alice
by Lisa Genova

The Hunger Games
by Suzanne Collins

The Devil in the White City
by Erik Larson

The Kitchen House
by Kathleen Grissom

Everything I Never Told You
by Celeste Ng

The Thirteenth Tale
by Diane Setterfield

The Boys in the Boat
by Daniel James Brown

**The Curious Incident of the
Dog in the Night-Time**
by Mark Haddon

The Great Alone
by Kristin Hannah

The Kite Runner
by Khaled Hosseini

All the Light We Cannot See
By Anthony Doerr

Birdsong
By Sebastian Faulks

The Remains of the Day
By Kazuo Ishiguro

The Great Gatsby
by F. Scott Fitzgerald

I Capture The Castle
by Dodie Smith

The Catcher in the Rye
by J.D. Salinger

Suggested Books I Might Like to Read

_____

_____

_____

_____

_____

_____

_____

_____

_____

_____

_____

_____

_____

_____

_____

_____

_____

_____

_____

_____

_____

_____

_____

Suggested Books I Might Like to Read

_____

_____

_____

_____

_____

_____

_____

_____

_____

_____

_____

_____

_____

_____

_____

_____

_____

_____

_____

_____

_____

_____

_____

Suggested Books I Might Like to Read

_____

_____

_____

_____

_____

_____

_____

_____

_____

_____

_____

_____

_____

_____

_____

_____

_____

_____

_____

_____

_____

_____

_____

MEMBERS

Book Club Members Contact Details

Name:

Number:

Address:

Other Infomation:

Name:

Number:

Address:

Other Infomation:

Name:

Number:

Address:

Other Infomation:

Name:

Number:

Address:

Other Infomation:

Book Club Members Contact Details

Name :

Number :

Address :

Other Infomation :

Name :

Number :

Address :

Other Infomation :

Name :

Number :

Address :

Other Infomation :

Name :

Number :

Address :

Other Infomation :

Book Club Members Contact Details

Name :

Number :

Address :

Other Infomation :

Name :

Number :

Address :

Other Infomation :

Name :

Number :

Address :

Other Infomation :

Name :

Number :

Address :

Other Infomation :

Book Club Members Contact Details

Name :

Number :

Address :

Other Infomation :

Name :

Number :

Address :

Other Infomation :

Name :

Number :

Address :

Other Infomation :

Name :

Number :

Address :

Other Infomation :

HOW TO
START A
BOOK CLUB

Tips on How to Start Your Own Book Club

Book clubs can broaden your reading repertoire and may even give you life long friends. If you haven't already joined one, here are a few tips for setting up your own book group.

Members

Book groups can have any number of members, from 2 to 20 the choice is yours. Although with large groups, it can be hard for everyone to contribute or find a space to meet. Eight is a good number then if a couple of members can't make it, you still have enough people for a good discussion.

Frequency

Meetings can be as frequent or infrequent as you like. Monthly meetings are popular as it gives everyone a chance to get hold of the book and time to read it. Also allocating the first Tuesday say, of the month, means people are more likely to remember the date and make all the meetings.

Book Choice

Letting each member pick a book, in turn, means you likely to read a wide range of authors and book genres. Ask members to choose a book they and no one else has already read. Consider if the title is in paperback, it may be cheaper or available to borrow from your local library.

Location

Try to find a quiet place to meet, such as at the members home whose book choice you just read. It works well if members turn up empty-handed and just the host provides drinks, nibbles or a light supper as and when it's their turn. Or some groups meet in a quiet pub a cafe or virtually online.

Structure

Your meetings can be as formal or relaxed as you want them to be. A good book group discussion is helped if the person who chooses the book brings along questions they have found online. Often the publisher and other websites will have book-specific questions already prepared to help keep the discussion flowing. At the end of the meeting, you might like to score the book using the questions in this book. Ideally, at this point, the next member will announce their book choice to read next month.

DISCUSSION
QUESTIONS

Book Discussion Ideas

The person who has nominated this month's book might like to start by saying why she/he chose it. That same person might lead the discussion with book-specific questions. (See over the page for suggested websites).

If you run out of discussion points, here are some ideas of what to talk about:

- Start with what was your reaction to the book - did you love it, loathe it or remain indifferent to it? Why?
- What is the book really about - the books themes, plot and topic?
- What other books did this remind you of? Was it unique?
- Comment on the quality of the writing, prose and plot structure.
- Did the book's pace seem too fast/too slow/just right?
- Were the characters real for you? Who do you sympathise with? Are the characters vividly portrayed and memorable?
- Is there a particularly memorable piece of writing or scene in the book?
- Does the book have a message?
- Did you learn anything from this book?
- What did you think of the book's length? If it's too long, what would you cut? If too short, what would you add?
- What did you think about the ending?
- What does it tell you about the author?
- If you could ask the author of one question, what would it be?
- If you were making a movie of this book, who would you cast?
- What do you think of the book's title? How does it relate to the book's contents? What other titles might you choose?
- What do you think of the book's cover? How well does it convey what the book is about?
- If it's a prizewinner, did it deserve to be?

Remember, the discussion can often be even more stimulating if you disliked a book (carefully expressed). Did you lose interest and why? Was it the characters or the story itself? Too confusing - or too obvious? Too much or not enough description?

Non-Fiction Question Ideas

Questions for a Memoir/Biography

- How much did you know about this person before reading the novel?
- How would you describe this person? What is their most impressive quality?
- Is there any particular aspect of their life that shocked or surprised you? Were there any parts of the book that did not ring true? Which?
- Were there any parts of the book/their life where you would have liked more information?
- Were there aspects of the book/their life that were too detailed? Which?
- Can this person write or is it just a great story? How much help do you think the author has had to write the book?

Questions for Non-fiction.

- What did you find surprising about the facts introduced in this book?
- How has reading this book changed your opinion of a certain person or topic?
- Does the author present information in a way that is interesting and insightful, and if so, how does he or she achieve this?
- If the author is writing on a debatable issue, does he or she give proper consideration to all sides of the debate?
- Does he or she seem to have a bias? Were the sources credible?
- How has the book increased your interest in the subject matter?

Resources for book specific discussion questions:

Search the publisher's website or Google 'Book Group discussion questions for....'name of the book'....' this is likely to bring up book specific questions. Questions may be found at:

www.goodreads.com

www.litlovers.com

www.bookbrowse.com

www.readinggroupguides.com

Printed in Great Britain
by Amazon

32403665R00053